Baby Hippos at the Zoo

Cecelia H. Brannon

Enslow Publishing
101 W. 23rd Street
Suite 240
New York, NY 10011
USA
enslow.com

Published in 2016 by Enslow Publishing, LLC.
101 W. 23rd Street, Suite 240, New York, NY 10011

Library of Congress Cataloging-in-Publication Data

Brannon, Cecelia H.
  Baby hippos at the zoo / by Cecelia H. Brannon.
    p. cm. — (All about baby zoo animals)
  Includes bibliographical references and index.
  ISBN 978-0-7660-7148-3 (library binding)
  ISBN 978-0-7660-7145-2 (pbk.)
  ISBN 978-0-7660-7146-9 (6-pack)
  1. Hippopotamus — Infancy — Juvenile literature. 2. Zoo animals — Juvenile literature. I. Brannon,
Cecelia H. II. Title.
  QL737.U57 B73 2016
  599.63'5139—d23

Printed in the United States of America

To Our Readers: We have done our best to make sure all website addresses in this book were active and
appropriate when we went to press. However, the author and the publisher have no control over and
assume no liability for the material available on those websites or on any websites they may link to.
Any comments or suggestions can be sent by e-mail to customerservice@enslow.com.

Photos Credits: Cover, p. 6 Henk Bentlage/Shutterstock.com; p. 1 Elliotte Rusty Harold/Shutterstock.
com; pp. 4–5 sunipix55/Shutterstock.com; pp. 3 (left), 8 © iStockphoto.com/Raats; p. 10 Handout/
Getty Images News/Getty Images; pp. 3 (right), 12 visa netpakdee/Shutterstock.com; p. 14 AAAR
Studio/Shutterstock.com; pp. 3 (center), 16 drferry/iStock/Thinkstock; p. 18 tanktrik71/Shutterstock.
com; p. 20 ylq/Shuttterstock.com; p. 22 abxyz/Shutterstock.com.

Contents

Words to Know

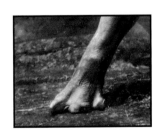

calf   herd   webbed

4

Who lives at the zoo?

A baby hippo lives at the zoo!

A baby hippo is called a calf.

A hippo calf has smooth brown skin. It has whiskers on its lips, ears, and tail.

A hippo calf has an extra eyelid that covers its eyes so it can see underwater. It also has webbed toes. These help the hippo swim.

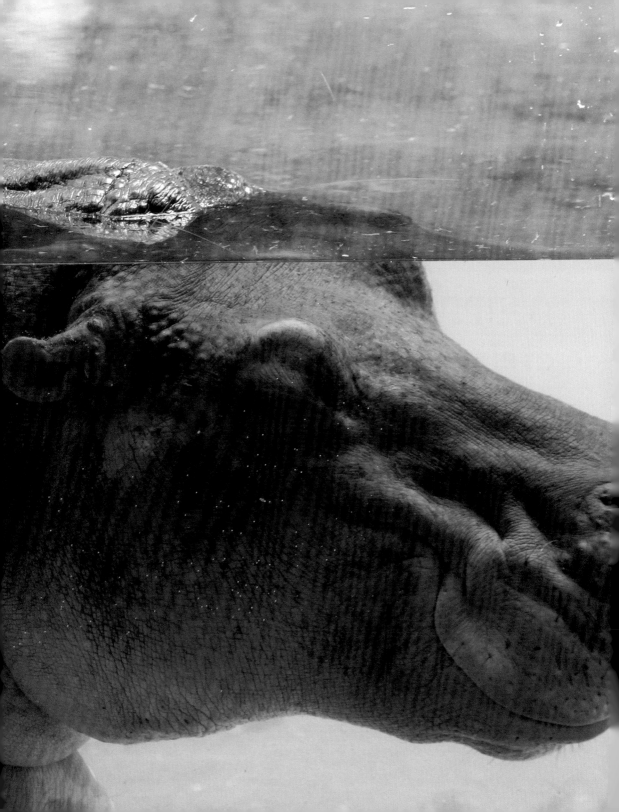

A hippo calf can sleep underwater. Its nose closes, and it bobs up for air.

A hippo calf lives in the zoo with its family. A group of hippos is called a herd or school.

A hippo calf eats grass, hay, vegetables, and fruit. It gets food from the zookeeper.

A hippo calf can make sounds both in water and on land. Its roar is very loud. It also makes snorts, grumbles, wheezes, and honks.

You can see a hippo calf at the zoo!

Read More

Borgert-Spaniol, Megan. *Baby Hippos*. Minneapolis, MN: Bellwether Media, Inc., 2015.

Owings, Lisa. *Meet a Baby Hippo*. New York: Lerner Publications, 2015.

Websites

San Diego Zoo Kids: Hippopotamus
zoo.sandiegozoo.org/animals/hippopotamus

National Geographic Kids: Hippopotamus
kids.nationalgeographic.com/animals/hippopotamus/

Index

Guided Reading Level: B
Guided Reading Leveling System is based on the guidelines recommended by Fountas and Pinnell.

Word Count: 145